Published by Creative Education
P.O. Box 227, Mankato, Minnesota 56002
Creative Education is an imprint of The Creative Company

Design and production by Blue Design
Printed in the United States of America

Photographs by Corbis (Bettmann, Amanda Hall/Robert Harding World Imagery, JESSICA RINALDI/Reuters), Getty Images (APA, Al Bello, Bruce Bennett Studios, Otto Greule Jr/Allsport, Andy Hayt, Hulton Archive, Carl Iwasaki//Time Life Pictures, Brad Mangin/MLB Photos, National Baseball Hall of Fame Library/MLB Photos, Gary Newkirk, Art Rickerby//Time Life Pictures, Photo File, Rich Pilling/MLB Photos, Joseph Scherschel//Time Life Pictures, Ezra Shaw, Rick Stewart, Ron Vesely/MLB Photos)

Library of Congress Cataloging-in-Publication Data

Nichols, John, 1966-
The story of the Boston Red Sox / by John Nichols.
p. cm. — (Baseball: the great American game)
Includes index.
ISBN-13: 978-1-58341-481-1
1. Boston Red Sox (Baseball team)—History—Juvenile literature. I. Title. II. Series.

GV875.B62N53 2007
796.357'640974461—dc22   2006027664

First Edition
9 8 7 6 5 4 3 2 1

Cover: Outfielder Carl Yastrzemski
Page 1: Pitcher Bill Dineen
Page 3: Pitcher Jonathan Papelbon

THE STORY OF THE
BOSTON RED SOX

by John Nichols

DAVID ORTIZ

THE STORY OF THE
Boston Red Sox

he burly slugger stood at the plate with his team's season hanging in the balance. It was the 12th inning of Game 4 of the 2004 American League Championship Series, and his team faced elimination by its bitter rival, the New York Yankees. The pitch came in fast, but after meeting designated hitter David Ortiz's bat, it left even faster, rocketing high over the right-field fence for the game-winning home run. At the time, it appeared Ortiz's blast would serve only to prevent his Boston Red Sox from being swept in four straight games by their long-time nemesis. As it turned out, Ortiz's clutch round-tripper sparked not only the greatest playoff comeback in major league baseball history but also the city's first World Series championship since 1918. For long-suffering Boston fans, the championship that had eluded them for decades had finally arrived.

BOSTON, CITY OF FIRSTS

**M**any of the English colonists who came to America in the early 1600s settled in the northeastern corner of the country, a region that later became known as New England. From that time until today, the city of Boston, Massachusetts, has served as the economic and cultural heart of the region. A major harbor town, Boston provides a business gateway to the world and also boasts some of the nation's finest schools, museums, and libraries.

Because Boston is one of the country's oldest cities, it features many American "firsts." Boston

BILL DINEEN – Dineen was the hero of the very first World Series (1903). He carried Boston to the championship by earning three pitching victories, two of them shutouts. After his playing days, he put his baseball knowledge to use as a longtime umpire.

BILL DINEEN

BOSTON – This historic city became a sports hotbed with the birth of the Red Sox more than a century ago. Boston has since been home to other successful pro teams as well, including basketball's Celtics, hockey's Bruins, and football's Patriots.

is home to the nation's first college, lighthouse, and newspaper. Fittingly, the city is also home to one of the nation's first and finest professional baseball franchises. In 1901, Major League Baseball's American League (AL) was born, and it chose Boston as the site of one of its charter franchises.

The AL's first commissioner, Ban Johnson, formed the new league to compete against the older, more-established National League (NL). Boston's first teams wore blue socks and were known by a variety of names such as the Pilgrims, Puritans, and Americans. The team wouldn't officially adopt the name "Red Sox" until 1908, when team owner John I. Taylor chose the name in honor of the team's brightly colored socks.

BAN JOHNSON – A former sportswriter, Johnson was a no-nonsense man who showed tough leadership and business savvy in turning the AL into a legitimate rival to the NL. He helped make the first World Series in 1903 (opposite) a reality.

BAN JOHNSON

1903 WORLD SERIES

PITCHER · CY YOUNG

Early in the career of Denton True Young, his fastball blew by so many hitters that fans and teammates began to call him "Cyclone." Over time, the nickname was shortened to "Cy," and forever afterward he would be known as Cy Young. During his 22-year career, Young started more than 800 games and pitched more than 7,000 innings without suffering a serious injury. His major-league record of 511 career victories is nearly 100 more than the second-best total. Today, baseball annually honors the best pitcher in each league with the Cy Young Award.

STATS

Red Sox seasons: 1901–08

Height: 6-2

Weight: 210

- **5 seasons of 30 or more wins**
- **749 complete games (most all-time)**
- **2,803 career strikeouts**
- **76 career shutouts**

CY YOUNG
PITCHER

BOSTON
RED SOX

Boston was a powerhouse in the early years of the AL. Led by star hurlers Denton "Cy" Young and Bill Dineen, Boston boasted one of the finest pitching staffs in baseball. Thirty-four years old when he joined the Boston team in 1901, Young had already spent many years in the NL. Some critics thought his illustrious career was coming to an end. Young proved them wrong, nailing down 192 of his major-league-record 511 total victories during his eight seasons in Boston. "At a time when most pitchers are winding down, Young was just getting started," said Boston manager Jimmy Collins. "His might be a record that may never be broken."

By 1903, the AL and NL had decided to end what had become a bitter rivalry and come together for a new kind of end-of-season contest. The AL champion Boston Pilgrims would face the NL champion Pittsburgh Pirates in a best-of-nine playoff series (now best-of-seven) that would become the first-ever World Series. Pittsburgh was heavily favored, but in a shocking upset, Boston won the series five games to three. The next year, Boston captured the AL title again, but there would be no World Series. Still upset over the NL's loss the year before, the owner of the NL champion New York Giants refused to play a World Series against the "inferior" American Leaguers.

THE ROYAL ROOTERS

During the 1903 season, a spirited group of Red Sox fans began to gather before games at a nearby pub. From there, they would walk to the game, playing instruments and singing. Before long, they came to be known as Boston's "Royal Rooters." During the ninth inning of Game 4 of the 1903 World Series, Boston trailed the Pittsburgh Pirates 5–1. Looking for a spark, the Royal Rooters began to sing a Broadway showtune called "Tessie" that had nothing to do with baseball but did unnerve the Pirates. Although they lost the game, the Sox rallied for three runs while the Rooters sang. Convinced they were on to something, the Royal Rooters sang the song during every game for the rest of the series, and Boston responded by sweeping all four contests on its way to the title. The Royal Rooters continued singing "Tessie" during all three of the Red Sox World Series victories in 1912, 1915, and 1916. By 1917, the group had disbanded, and the singing stopped. Prior to the 2004 season, the Red Sox commissioned a local band to create a new version of "Tessie," which the team played during every game of its World Series championship season.

JOE WOOD

A DYNASTY GROWS IN FENWAY

he World Series returned in 1905, but it took a few years for the Red Sox to earn their way back to the championship. By the next decade, the team had undergone several changes. A new group of stars had taken the stage for Boston, and the team had moved into the home it still has to this day—Fenway Park.

Leading the charge for the re-tooled Red Sox were pitcher "Smokey" Joe Wood and outfielders Tris Speaker, Duffy Lewis, and Harry Hopper. The hard-throwing Wood debuted with the Red Sox in 1908, and by 1912 he was "the closest thing to unhittable I've ever seen," according to Philadelphia Athletics second baseman Eddie Collins. Speaker was perhaps the greatest center fielder of his time. Incredibly fast and blessed with a cannon of an arm, "Spoke," as his teammates called him, played a shallow outfield but rarely had a ball hit over his head. "Most hits in a game land in front of outfielders, so I figured it was the smart place to play," explained Speaker. On offense, Speaker's speed and power anchored a lineup that scored runs in bunches.

In 1914, the Red Sox added 19-year-old pitcher George "Babe" Ruth to the

"Smokey" Joe Wood was famous for his scorching fastball before a thumb injury in 1913 slowed him down.

CATCHER · JASON VARITEK

A natural leader, Varitek was named team captain in 2004, becoming only the third in Red Sox history. A fiery competitor, the big catcher was known for his constant hustle. He was also known for a scuffle with New York Yankees slugger Alex Rodriguez at home plate in 2004, when Rodriguez threatened a Red Sox pitcher after being hit by a ball. Varitek's willingness to stand up for his pitcher endeared him to fans and teammates alike. One of the better hitting catchers in the major leagues, the switch-hitting Varitek was a long-ball threat from either side of the plate.

STATS

Red Sox seasons: 1997–present

Height: 6-2

Weight: 210

- **2005 Gold Glove winner**
- **3 seasons of 20 or more HR**
- **2-time All-Star**
- **Career-best 25 HR in 2003**

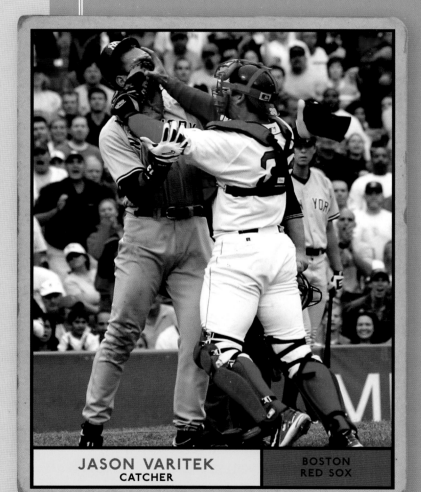

JASON VARITEK
CATCHER

BOSTON
RED SOX

TRIS SPEAKER

Tris Speaker was the greatest doubles hitter of all time, collecting a major-league record 793 two-baggers.

squad. By 1916, Ruth was a 20-game winner and one of the best hurlers in the league. But he really impressed fans with his ability to hit. In an era in which home runs were rare because of the lack of jump in the ball, the Babe showed an uncanny knack for hitting round-trippers. In 1919, he would hit 29 home runs—a figure that was better than the total home runs hit by five of the AL's eight teams put together!

The mighty Red Sox captured World Series championships in 1912, 1915, 1916, and 1918, defeating the New York Giants, Philadelphia Phillies, Brooklyn Robins, and Chicago Cubs, respectively. The Red Sox were truly a dynasty, but even though they were a major success on the field, they started to have problems off of it. By the end of the 1919 season, Ruth had become a distraction. He constantly squabbled with the team over money, and his desire to play in the outfield rather than pitch irritated his teammates.

The prospect of giving Ruth a big raise, coupled with Red Sox owner Harry Frazee's personal debts, prompted Frazee to sell the Babe to the New York Yankees for $125,000. This trade may have helped solve his financial problems, but it signaled the end of the Red Sox dynasty. A popular legend has it that, upon leaving Boston, Ruth put a hex on the Sox to make sure they would never win a World Series without him. Whether magic or myth, the "Curse of the Bambino," as the hex came to be known, would seem to haunt the Red Sox for decades.

Nicknamed "The Bambino" and "The Sultan of Swat," Babe Ruth quickly became a baseball icon.

"SPLENDID SPLINTER" HITS THE SOX

Frazee's sale of Ruth proved to be the biggest blow in the demolition of the Red Sox dynasty, but it was not the only one. The owner made a steady practice of trading or selling off great players such as shortstop Everett Scott and pitcher Carl Mays. By the early 1920s, the Red Sox's few remaining stars, such as first baseman Earl Webb and pitcher Howard Ehmke, were not able to keep the team in contention. Boston fell into the AL cellar and stayed there for nearly 20 years.

The team's fortunes finally started to improve in the mid-1930s, when Thomas A. Yawkey purchased the team. Yawkey loved baseball and was committed to improving the downtrodden Sox. He actively traded for and bought top stars such as shortstop Joe Cronin, first baseman Jimmie Foxx, and pitchers Wes Farrell and Lefty Grove. Under Yawkey, the Red Sox also developed some great players of their own, including hard-hitting second baseman Bobby Doerr and outfielder Ted Williams.

The tall, skinny Williams didn't look like much when he came to the Red Sox in 1939, but his outstanding play quickly earned him the nickname "The

FIRST BASEMAN · MO VAUGHN

Vaughn was one of the most feared hitters in baseball during the 1990s, and his trademark high-rising home runs made him a favorite among Red Sox fans. Known as "The Hit Dog," the left-handed slugger always stood close to the plate with his arms holding the bat high overhead. Leaning over the plate, Vaughn dared pitchers to throw inside, where his quick wrists and incredible strength turned fastballs into long balls. Vaughn was also a great competitor whose vocal style and boisterous personality endeared him to teammates and fans.

STATS

Red Sox seasons: 1991–98

Height: 6-1

Weight: 230

- **1995 AL MVP**
- **3-time All-Star**
- **1996 AL RBI leader (126)**
- **Career-best 44 HR in 1996**

MO VAUGHN
FIRST BASEMAN

BOSTON
RED SOX

JOHNNY PESKY

THE PESKY POLE

Shortstop Johnny Pesky was one of the all-time greatest Red Sox players. He was a superb fielder, and his lifetime .307 batting average is a testament to his hitting skill, but at 5-foot-9 and 165 pounds, he was never known as a long-ball threat. During his 10 years in Boston during the 1940s and '50s, Pesky hit only 17 home runs, and only 6 of them were at Fenway Park. On the rare occasion when he did hit a home run in Fenway, Pesky's "shots" just barely slipped over the three-foot-tall right-field fence, directly next to the foul pole—a mere 302 feet away from home plate. While broadcasting a Red Sox game decades later, former Red Sox pitcher Mel Parnell witnessed someone else imitating Pesky's unusual style of banking a homer off the right-field foul pole. Parnell jokingly dubbed the tall yellow marker the "Pesky Pole," in honor of his former teammate. The nickname stuck, memorializing both Johnny Pesky and his pole. Today, more than 50 years after Pesky hit his last home run, a hitter who hooks a ball around the right-field foul pole in Fenway Park has "wrapped one around the Pesky Pole."

Splendid Splinter." Williams combined keen vision, knowledge of the strike zone, and perhaps the most graceful left-handed swing the game had ever seen to produce incredible offensive numbers. In 1941, Williams posted a .406 batting average, making him the most recent player to hit .400 or better for a season. By the end of his career, Williams had hit 521 home runs and owned a .344 lifetime average. "All I want out of life," he once said, "is that when I walk down the street, folks will say, 'there goes the greatest hitter who ever lived.'"

In the early '40s, Williams and several of Boston's other stars left the game to serve their country in World War II. In 1946, after the war ended, they returned and led Boston to the AL pennant. In addition to Williams and Doerr, the team featured speedy outfielder Dom DiMaggio, slick-fielding shortstop Johnny Pesky, and hard-throwing pitcher Dave "Boo" Ferriss. In the World Series, the Red Sox faced the St. Louis Cardinals. The series went a full seven games, but the Cardinals prevailed, winning 4–3 in the final contest.

The Red Sox would not make the playoffs for the rest of the 1940s and '50s. While always a good team, the Red Sox consistently finished behind the great New York Yankees teams of the time, a fact that added fuel to the already intense rivalry. "We'd win 80 games, they would win 90. We'd win 90 games, they would win 100," explained Boston catcher Sammy White. "No matter what we did, the Yankees always seemed to do just a little bit more."

that Sox fans started to refer to it as the "Impossible Dream" season. Unfortunately, the dream ended badly. The Red Sox's miraculous trip to the World Series ended in defeat, as the St. Louis Cardinals again got the best of them in seven games.

In 1969, Major League Baseball switched to divisional play (meaning both leagues were split into two divisions), and in 1975, the Red Sox stormed to their first AL Eastern Division title. Yaz remained the team's heart and soul, but Boston had also bolstered its lineup with young stars such as catcher Carlton Fisk and outfielders Jim Rice, Fred Lynn, and Dwight Evans. In the playoffs, the resurgent Red Sox knocked off the Oakland A's in the AL Championship Series (ALCS) and faced the Cincinnati Reds in the World Series. The series would prove to be one of high drama. In fact, the outcome was still up in the air until the ninth inning of Game 7, when the Reds pushed across a run in the top of the inning that the Red Sox could not answer. The Reds won the game and the series 4–3.

Boston contended for the AL East title again in 1978. After finishing the regular season tied with the New York Yankees, the two teams played a one-game playoff at Fenway Park. Late in the game, light-hitting Yankees shortstop Bucky Dent popped a fly ball over the Green Monster for a three-run homer to give the Yankees a lead they would not relinquish. The Red Sox fell short once again.

THE GREEN MONSTER

Fenway Park's tall left-field wall has been a part of the stadium since it opened in 1912. "The Green Monster," as it has come to be known, looms a mere 310 feet from home plate and stands 37 feet tall. What many people don't know is that at one time, the Green Monster wasn't green, and it wasn't such a monstrosity. Prior to 1934, the fence stood only 25 feet high, and before 1947, the fence wasn't green but was instead covered with advertisements. The Red Sox chose to raise the fence and put netting on top of it to protect the windows of buildings on Landsdowne Street from home run balls. The dark green paint first appeared during a stadium renovation. The tall wall has intrigued fans and players alike for decades and in some cases has confused its first-time viewers. When rookie pitcher Bill Lee joined the team in 1969, a veteran asked him if he'd ever seen Fenway Park. Lee had not, so the veteran walked him out on the field and asked him what he thought of the Green Monster. The inexperienced pitcher gawked at the wall, then turned to the veteran and asked, "Do they leave that up during the game?"

THIRD BASEMAN · WADE BOGGS

A student of hitting technique, Boggs was perhaps the best two-strike hitter who ever lived. He patiently took pitches and fouled off others, sizing up the pitcher's delivery with each throw, before calmly slashing a line drive into Fenway's outfield. An eight-time All-Star with the Sox, Boggs was a firm believer in routine. He ate chicken before every game and had a pre-game regimen of drills and exercises from which he never strayed. Only an adequate fielder when he arrived in the big leagues, Boggs tirelessly worked on his fielding until he eventually became a two-time Gold Glove winner.

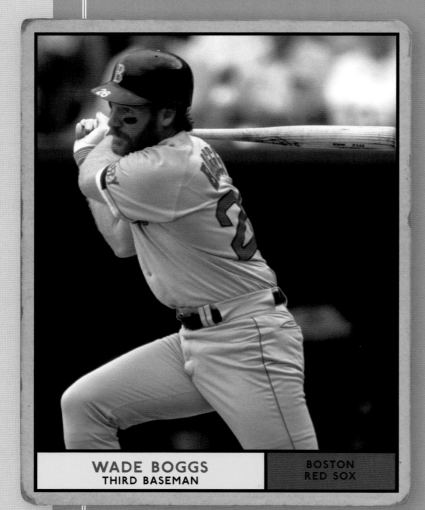

WADE BOGGS
THIRD BASEMAN

BOSTON
RED SOX

STATS

Red Sox seasons: 1982–92

Height: 6-2

Weight: 197

- **.328 career BA**
- **3,010 career hits**
- **1,513 career runs scored**
- **Baseball Hall of Fame inductee (2005)**

FISK WAVES IT FAIR

Game-winning home runs are always exciting, but game-winning home runs in the World Series instantly become part of baseball history. Red Sox catcher Carlton Fisk provided one of the game's most dramatic moments when he faced the Cincinnati Reds' Pat Darcy in Game 6 of the 1975 World Series. It was the 12th inning, and the score was knotted 6–6 when Fisk launched a Darcy pitch high and deep down the left-field line at Fenway Park. At first, it looked like the ball would hook foul, but Fisk, who was watching the flight of the ball from home plate, famously jumped and waved his arms, desperately willing the ball fair. As Red Sox fans held their breath, the ball ricocheted off the foul pole for a home run. Fisk's blast won the game and sent the series to a deciding seventh contest the next night. The Reds ended up winning Game 7 and the series, but more people will remember only Fisk's heroic home run and willful wave, a moment that *TV Guide* claimed in 1998 was "the greatest moment in the history of sports television."

ROGER CLEMENS

BOGGS AND THE ROCKET BLAST OFF

After Yastrzemski's retirement following the 1983 season, the team turned to a new group of stars for leadership. In the mid-1980s, Boston was anchored by third baseman Wade Boggs, left fielder Mike Greenwell, and hard-throwing pitcher Roger Clemens. Boggs was not a power hitter, but his uncanny ability to spray line drives all over the field made him equally as dangerous. During his career in Boston, Boggs would capture five AL batting titles and make eight All-Star Games.

Clemens gave Boston what it had lacked for years—a power pitching ace. Known to fans as "The Rocket" due to the eye-popping velocity of his fastball, Clemens also subscribed to the old school of pitching that dictated that all batters who looked too comfortable at the plate ended up on the seat of their pants—thanks to a hard inside pitch from the Rocket. "Roger is a good guy, but when he is pitching, hitters are not just opponents, they are the enemy," said Red Sox catcher Rich Gedman.

In 1986, Clemens won 24 games, and Boggs hit .357 to lead Boston to the AL East title. After advancing to the

Roger Clemens topped the 20-win mark three times during his Sox career and won three Cy Young Awards.

World Series with an ALCS win over the Los Angeles Angels, Boston jumped out to a three-games-to-two lead over the New York Mets. Game 6 in New York went into extra innings, but with two outs in the bottom of the 10th, Boston led 5–3. Then, with only one out separating the Sox from a championship, disaster struck: Boston gave up three singles, threw a wild pitch, and first baseman Bill Buckner committed an error on a slow-rolling ground ball, all of which combined to give the Mets three runs and the victory. In Game 7, the Mets finished off the reeling Sox 8–5 to win the series. "This game breaks your heart," said Red Sox right fielder Dwight Evans. "I've been around a long time, but I've never seen anything like this."

With the help of Boggs and Clemens, the Red Sox remained a contender for the rest of the decade, but the team never returned to the World Series. After finishing at the bottom of the division in 1992, Boston began to rebuild with new stars such as first baseman Mo Vaughn, whose 39 homers and 126 RBI in 1995 earned him the AL Most Valuable Player (MVP) award. But even with Vaughn, the Red Sox were not able to get over the hump. By the end of the '90s, Boggs, Clemens, and Vaughn had all left as free agents, and the Red Sox were again looking to rebuild.

SHORTSTOP · NOMAR GARCIAPARRA

Garciaparra's unusual first name is actually his father's name, Ramon, spelled backwards. His unique name signaled from the beginning that he was a rare talent. A powerful hitter, the California native belted 30 home runs during his first full season in the majors. Garciaparra also wowed fans with his strong arm, throwing out base runners from places other shortstops only dreamed about. Perhaps the trait that most endeared him to Red Sox fans, though, was his constant hustle. Whether beating out an infield hit or ranging deep in the hole to snare a tough grounder, Garciaparra always gave his all.

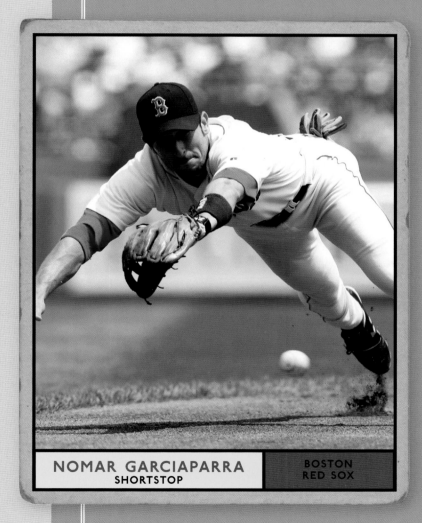

NOMAR GARCIAPARRA
SHORTSTOP
BOSTON
RED SOX

STATS

Red Sox seasons: 1996–2004

Height: 6-0

Weight: 190

- **1997 AL Rookie of the Year**
- **6-time All-Star**
- **1997 AL hits leader (209)**
- **7 seasons with 20 or more HR**

MANNY RAMIREZ – Although sometimes accused of laziness and half-hearted fielding effort, Ramirez was one of the most dangerous hitters of the late 1990s and early 2000s. In his first six Boston seasons, he averaged 39 homers and 118 RBI a year.

CHAMPIONS AT LAST

By 2002, the Red Sox began to take on a new look. Shortstop Nomar Garciaparra, slugging outfielder Manny Ramirez, and pitcher Pedro Martinez formed the heart and soul of the team. Garciaparra rose quickly through Boston's minor-league system and made his debut with the Red Sox in 1996. An excellent fielder who hit for both power and a high average, Garciaparra also displayed a flair for making big, game-altering plays. Ramirez came to Boston as a free agent from the Cleveland Indians. An offensive machine, he excelled at hitting with runners on base, consistently ranking among the league's RBI leaders. The hard-throwing Martinez led Boston on the defensive side. Coming to the Red Sox via a trade with the Montreal Expos, Martinez was small in stature (5-foot-11 and 170 pounds) but possessed a big fastball and brought a confident swagger to the mound.

In 2003, the Red Sox made it to the postseason before the Curse of the Bambino struck again. In Game 7 of the ALCS between the Sox and the Yankees, third baseman Aaron Boone hit a home run in the bottom of the 11th to win the game and the series for New York.

Prior to the 2004 campaign, Boston signed star pitcher Curt Schilling

David Ortiz had a knack for late-inning heroics, hitting two walk-off home runs during the 2004 playoffs.

DAVID ORTIZ

SCHILLING'S RED SOCK

Things did not look good for the Red Sox during the 2004 ALCS. Down three games to two against their bitter rival, the New York Yankees, the Sox sent Curt Schilling to the mound for Game 6. Normally one of the game's best hurlers, Schilling had torn a tendon in his ankle prior to the series, and it hampered his delivery. Pitching against the Yankees in Game 1, he was roughed up for six runs in three innings. Before Game 6, team doctors tried to secure the injured tendon by stitching it to Schilling's skin. In obvious pain, Schilling took the mound and gutted out seven strong innings.

Midway through his performance, Schilling's stitches ruptured, and blood soaked through his uniform sock. Schilling's courageous pitching inspired fans and teammates alike, and the Sox went on to defeat the Yankees 4–2. Just five days later, a re-stitched Schilling took the mound again, this time facing the St. Louis Cardinals in Game 2 of the World Series. He performed masterfully, getting the win while giving up only one run in six innings. Many Red Sox fans cited Schilling's iron-willed feats as the keys to Boston's stunning postseason success that year.

LEFT FIELDER · TED WILLIAMS

Arguably the greatest hitter who ever lived, Williams's keen eyesight allowed him to "pick out the stitches" on the ball as it was delivered. Williams's greatness was on full display during his two Triple Crown seasons in 1942 and 1946, when he led the league in home runs, RBI, and batting average. Despite losing nearly five years of his career to military service in World War II and the Korean War, Williams's career offensive numbers rank among the game's all-time greatest. In an ending fitting for the hero he was, Williams blasted a home run in the last at bat of his career.

STATS

Red Sox seasons: 1939–42, 1946–60

Height: 6-3

Weight: 205

- **17-time All-Star**
- **521 career HR**
- **.344 lifetime BA**
- **Baseball Hall of Fame inductee (1966)**

TED WILLIAMS
LEFT FIELDER

BOSTON
RED SOX

CENTER FIELDER · DOM DiMAGGIO

Known as the "Little Professor" because of his glasses and small stature, DiMaggio played in the shadow of his more famous teammate, Ted Williams, and his brother, New York Yankees star Joe DiMaggio. Quiet and unassuming, Dom DiMaggio was a great player in his own right. Swift and sure-handed, he effortlessly tracked down rockets that looked to be sure hits. Red Sox fans joked that DiMaggio had to play both center and left field to cover for the slow-footed Williams. At the plate, DiMaggio was a superb leadoff hitter and base runner who once put together a 34-game hitting streak.

STATS

Red Sox seasons: 1940–42, 1946–53

Height: 5-9

Weight: 168

- **7-time All-Star**

- **.298 career BA**

- **1,680 career hits**

- **2-time AL leader in runs scored**

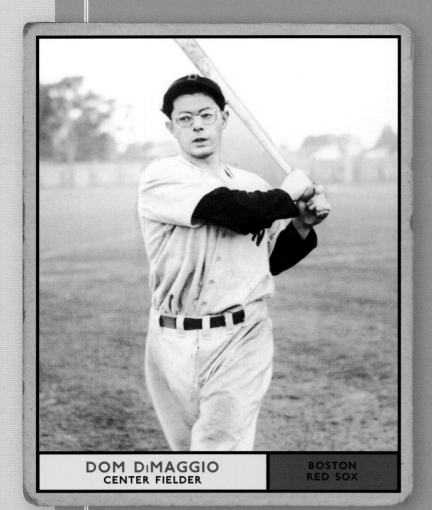

DOM DiMAGGIO
CENTER FIELDER

BOSTON
RED SOX

from the Arizona Diamondbacks. The season seemed to be in jeopardy early on, however, when an unhappy Garciaparra was traded away to the Chicago Cubs. Many experts thought Boston was doomed after the loss of its star shortstop, but the Red Sox thought differently. Thanks to extraordinary performances by Schilling, Ramirez, and designated hitter David Ortiz, Boston again rallied to make the postseason as the AL Wild Card team.

After quickly dispatching of the Anaheim Angels in the Division Series, the Red Sox again faced the Yankees in the ALCS. New York started fast, winning the first three games of the series. On the brink of another playoff defeat at the hands of the Yankees, Boston trailed 4–3 late in Game 4 before rallying to tie the contest in the bottom of the ninth. The game remained tied until the bottom of the 12th, when Ortiz belted a dramatic two-run homer to win the game. Given new life, the Sox won Game 5 on another Ortiz homer in extra innings. Inspired by the big slugger's exploits and boosted by fans' frenzied support, Boston rolled to victories in Games 6 and 7, becoming the first team ever to come back from a three-games-to-zero deficit to win a playoff series.

Riding high, the Red Sox faced another old nemesis in the World Series— the St. Louis Cardinals. But this time there would be no suspense. Boston

PEDRO MARTINEZ

Pedro Martinez used a wide pitch assortment, mixed speeds, and varied throwing angles to bewilder hitters.

RIGHT FIELDER · DWIGHT EVANS

One of the greatest right fielders of any era, "Dewey," as he was known, could field any hit well. Base runners often stopped dead in their tracks when the ball was hit to him. Evans also had a knack for making dramatic catches. His leaping grab of a would-be home run late in Game 6 of the 1975 World Series saved the game, if not the series, for the Red Sox.

Over his 19 seasons in Boston, Red Sox fans grew to rely on the durable Evans's remarkable productivity. He hit 20 or more home runs in 11 seasons.

STATS

Red Sox seasons: 1972–90

Height: 6-2

Weight: 205

- **3-time All-Star**
- **8-time Gold Glove winner**
- **385 career HR**
- **2,446 career hits**

DWIGHT EVANS
RIGHT FIELDER

BOSTON
RED SOX

RETIRED NUMBERS

Retiring a player's number is the greatest honor a team can bestow upon one of its former stars. By saying that no other player will ever wear a particular number again, it means that the honored player's greatness will be remembered forever. Many famous players have worn the uniform of the Boston Red Sox, but only a few have been given the honor of having their numbers retired by the team. The Red Sox have two requirements a player must meet in order for his number to be retired: He must first have been elected to the Baseball Hall of Fame, and he must have played at least 10 seasons for the Red Sox. More than 1,600 players have worn a Red Sox uniform, but only six numbers have been retired by the Red Sox: Bobby Doerr's #1, Joe Cronin's #4, Carl Yastrzemski's #8, Ted Williams's #9, Carlton Fisk's #27, and Jackie Robinson's #42. Robinson, a Brooklyn Dodgers great of the 1940s and '50s, never played for the Red Sox, but his outstanding career and achievement in becoming the first African American to play in the major leagues earned him the honor of having his number retired throughout major league baseball in 1997.

MANAGER · JOE CRONIN

The winningest manager in Red Sox history, Cronin guided Boston to 1,071 wins during his 13 seasons at the helm. Cronin was one of the last player/managers in the major leagues. An excellent shortstop, he carried a .301 lifetime batting average. Cronin came to the Red Sox in 1935, when team owner Tom Yawkey purchased him from the Washington Senators for the then-astronomical figure of $250,000. After retiring as manager of the Red Sox in 1947, Cronin served as the team's general manager before going on to become the first former player to be named a league president.

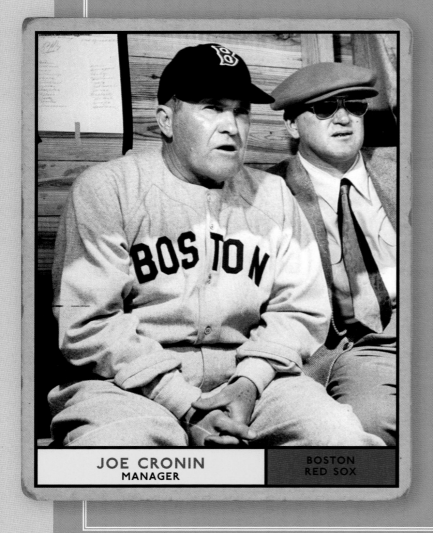

JOE CRONIN
MANAGER

BOSTON
RED SOX

STATS

Red Sox seasons as manager: 1935–47

Height: 5-11

Weight: 180

Managerial Record: 1,236–1,055

AL Pennant: 1946

Baseball Hall of Fame inductee (1956)

crushed the Cardinals in four straight games to capture its first title since 1918 and end the Curse of the Bambino. "This [victory] is for Ted Williams, Yaz, and all the other great players who made this franchise what it is today," said an emotional Schilling. "We are all proud to wear this uniform."

The next two seasons were disappointments in Boston. The Red Sox made the postseason as the AL Wild Card in 2005 but lost to the Chicago White Sox. Then, in 2006, Boston slipped out of the playoff picture with an 86–76 record. The team's drop was due in part to the departures of such stars as Martinez and center fielder Johnny Damon, but hopes for 2007 went up when the Red Sox added sensational Japanese pitcher Daisuke Matsuzaka to a roster that already featured talented young pitchers Josh Beckett and Jonathan Papelbon. "I'm very excited," said Boston general manager Theo Epstein. "This has a chance to be a pretty special club."

For more than 100 years, the Boston Red Sox have given their faithful fans a history full of championship victories, heartbreaking defeats, curses, and even a green monster. More than just the hometown team, the Red Sox have become a rooting obsession for all of New England. The day will come when others will join the league of Red Sox heroes, and when they do, the team's forever-loyal fans will be there to cheer them on: "Go, Sox! Go!"

All-Star Game 31
AL batting championships 25, 31
AL Championship Series 5, 26, 32, 35, 38, 41
AL Division Series 41
AL Eastern Division championships 26, 31
AL pennant 23, 46
AL Wild Card 41, 47
Baseball Hall of Fame 24, 28, 39, 46
Beckett, Josh 47
Boggs, Wade 28, 31, 32
Buckner, Bill 32
Clemens, Roger 31, 32
Collins, Jimmy 11
Conigliaro, Tony 25
Cronin, Joe 20, 45, 46
"Curse of the Bambino" 19, 35, 47
Cy Young Award 10
Damon, Johnny 47
DiMaggio, Dom 23, 40
Dineen, Bill 11
Doerr, Bobby 20, 23, 24, 45
Ehmke, Howard 20
Epstein, Theo 47
Evans, Dwight 26, 32, 43
Farrell, Wes 20
Fenway Park 15, 22, 25, 26, 27, 28, 29
 Green Monster 25, 26, 27
Ferriss, Dave 23
first team names 8
Fisk, Carlton 26, 29, 45
Fox, Jimmie 20
Frazee, Harry 19, 20
Garciaparra, Nomar 33, 35, 41
Gedman, Rich 31
Gold Glove award 16, 28, 43
Greenwell, Mike 31
Grove, Lefty 20
Hopper, Harry 15

Johnson, Ban 8
Lee, Bill 27
Lewis, Duffy 15
Lonborg, Jim 25
Lynn, Fred 26
major-league records 10
Martinez, Pedro 35, 47
Matsuzaka, Daisuke 47
Mays, Carl 20
MVP award 21, 32
Ortiz, David 5, 41
Papelbon, Jonathan 47
Parnell, Mel 22
Pesky, Johnny 22, 23
Ramirez, Manny 35, 41
retired numbers 45
Rice, Jim 26
Rookie of the Year award 33
"Royal Rooters" 13
Ruth, Babe 15, 19, 20
Schilling, Curt 35, 38, 41, 47
Scott, Everett 20
Scott, George 25
Speaker, Tris 15
Taylor, John I. 8
team captains 16
Triple Crown winners 25, 39
Varitek, Jason 16
Vaughn, Mo 21, 32
Webb, Earl 20
White, Sammy 23
Williams, Ted 20, 23, 25, 39, 40, 45, 47
Wood, Joe 15
world championships 5, 13, 19, 47
World Series 5, 11, 13, 15, 19, 23, 26, 29, 32, 38, 41, 43
Yastrzemski, Carl 25, 26, 31, 45, 47
Yawkey, Thomas A. 20, 46
Young, Cy 10, 11